**Put Beginning Readers on the Right Track with
ALL ABOARD READING™**

The All Aboard Reading series is especially designed for beginning readers. Written by noted authors and illustrated in full color, these are books that children really want to read—books to excite their imagination, expand their interests, make them laugh, and support their feelings. With fiction and nonfiction stories that are high interest and curriculum-related, All Aboard Reading books offer something for every young reader. And with four different reading levels, the All Aboard Reading series lets you choose which books are most appropriate for your children and their growing abilities.

Picture Readers
Picture Readers have super-simple texts, with many nouns appearing as rebus pictures. At the end of each book are 24 flash cards—on one side is a rebus picture; on the other side is the written-out word.

Station Stop 1
Station Stop 1 books are best for children who have just begun to read. Simple words and big type make these early reading experiences more comfortable. Picture clues help children to figure out the words on the page. Lots of repetition throughout the text helps children to predict the next word or phrase—an essential step in developing word recognition.

Station Stop 2
Station Stop 2 books are written specifically for children who are reading with help. Short sentences make it easier for early readers to understand what they are reading. Simple plots and simple dialogue help children with reading comprehension.

Station Stop 3
Station Stop 3 books are perfect for children who are reading alone. With longer text and harder words, these books appeal to children who have mastered basic reading skills. More complex stories captivate children who are ready for more challenging books.

In addition to All Aboard Reading books, look for All Aboard Math Readers™ (fiction stories that teach math concepts children are learning in school) and All Aboard Science Readers™ (nonfiction books that explore the most fascinating science topics in age-appropriate language).

All Aboard for happy reading!

Library of Congress Cataloging-in-Publication Data
Herman, John, 1944-
   Red, white, and blue : the story of the American flag / by John Herman ; illustrated by Robin Roraback.
      p.   cm.—(All aboard reading. Level 2)
   Summary : Describes how the American flag came into being, how it has changed over the years, and its importance as the symbol of our country.
   1. Flags—United States—Juvenile literature. [1. Flags—United States.]
   I. Roraback, Robin, ill. II. Title. III. Series.
CR113.H397 1998
929.9'2'0973—dc21   97-33413
                                                                                               CIP
ISBN 0-448-41270-5   H I J   AC

Red, White, and Blue
★ The Story of the American Flag ★

By John Herman

Illustrated by Robin Roraback

Grosset & Dunlap • New York

We all know the American flag.

Its bright colors fly at baseball games.

It flies at Fourth of July parades.

We even see it on clothes!

Our flag has lots of nicknames—

like Old Glory and

the Red, White, and Blue.

Sometimes it's called

the Stars and Stripes.

But where did our flag come from?

Who decided what it would look like?

The truth is that no one knows for sure.

Back in the 1700s,

America didn't have a flag.

It didn't need one.

It wasn't even a country yet.

8

It was just thirteen colonies.

The colonies belonged to England.

The English flag flew in towns from

New Hampshire to Georgia.

9

But as time went on,

the thirteen colonies didn't want

to belong to England anymore.

Americans decided to fight

for their freedom.

A war began.

It was the American Revolution.

Now a new flag was needed—

an American flag.

Who made our first flag?

Some people say it was

a woman named Betsy Ross.

Maybe you've heard of her.

Betsy Ross owned a sewing shop

in Philadelphia.

She was famous for her sewing.

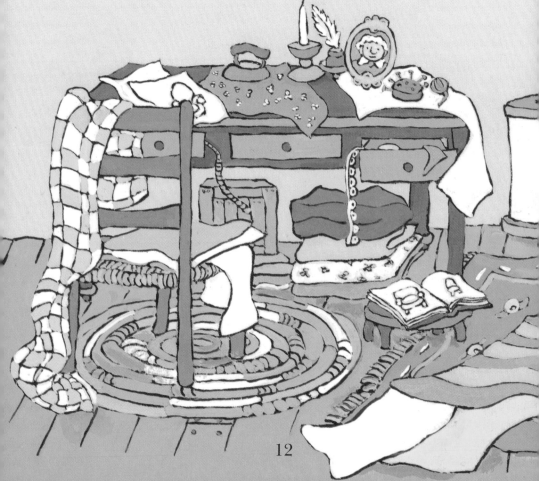

The story is that

one day a general came to see her.

The general was George Washington.

He was the head of the American army.

General Washington wanted a new flag.

It would make his soldiers feel

like a real army fighting for a real country.

He wanted Betsy Ross to make this flag.

He drew a picture of what he wanted.

Betsy Ross made some changes.

Then she showed the picture

to General Washington.

He liked it!

Betsy Ross sewed the flag.

And that was the very first

Stars and Stripes.

That is the story—and it's a good one.

But is it true?

Betsy Ross's grandson said it was.

He said that Betsy told him the story

when he was a little boy

and she was an old woman of eighty-four.

But there is no proof for this story.

So what do we know <u>for sure</u>?

We know that during the Revolution,
the colonists used lots of different flags.

But once the colonies became
the United States of America,
the country needed <u>one</u> flag—
the same flag for everybody.

So on June 14, 1777,

a decision was made.

The flag was going to have

thirteen red and white stripes.

The flag was also going to have

thirteen white stars

on a blue background,

one for each of the thirteen colonies.

Now the United States had a flag.

Congress had picked the colors

and the stars and stripes.

But Congress did not say where

the stars and stripes had to go.

So the flag still did not always

look the same!

People could put them
any way they liked.
Sometimes the stripes were
up and down, like this.

Sometimes the stars were
in a circle, like this.

But nobody minded.

Up and down or side to side,

the stars and stripes

still stood for the United States.

Over the years,

the flag became more and more

important to people.

In 1812, the United States was

at war with England again.

British soldiers came to America.

They sailed up our rivers.

They marched down our streets.
They even burned down
the White House—
the home of the president.

On the night
of September 13, 1814,
British soldiers bombed
a fort in Maryland.
All that night a man
watched the fighting.
His name was Francis Scott Key.
He was afraid.
What if the American soldiers
in the fort gave up?

But in the early morning light,

he saw the Stars and Stripes.

It was still flying above the fort!

He knew American soldiers

had won the battle.

Key felt very proud.

He wrote a poem

about the flag on the fort.

The poem was

"The Star-Spangled Banner."

Later the poem was put to music.

This song about our flag became

a song for our whole country.

The flag that Francis Scott Key saw
had fifteen stripes and fifteen stars.

Why?
Because by then
there were two more states—
Vermont and Kentucky.

Our country was getting bigger.

People were heading out west.

In time, more places

were going to want to be states.

Soon there would be too many

stripes to fit on the flag!

Congress had to do something.

So in 1818 this is what was decided:

The flag would go back to

thirteen red and white stripes.

And in the blue box

would be one white star for each state.

Every time there was a new state,

a new star would be added.

The United States in 1850

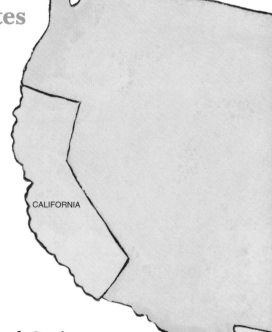

This map shows all the states as of 1850.

CALIFORNIA

At last the Stars and Stripes

looked the same everywhere it flew.

And Americans were proud of their flag.

They took the flag with them

as they moved west.

The flag crossed the Mississippi River

and the great grassy plains

and the Rocky Mountains.

It made it all the way to California.

Mississippi River

WISCONSIN

IOWA

MICHIGAN

ILLINOIS

INDIANA   OHIO

MISSOURI

KENTUCKY

ARKANSAS

TENNESSEE

MISSISSIPPI

ALABAMA

GEORGIA

TEXAS

LOUISIANA

FLORIDA

NEW HAMPSHIRE   MAINE

VERMONT

MASSACHUSETTS

NEW YORK   RHODE ISLAND

CONNECTICUT

PENNSYLVANIA

NEW JERSEY

DELAWARE

MARYLAND

VIRGINIA

NORTH
CAROLINA

SOUTH
CAROLINA

More and more states

were added to the country.

And more and more stars

were added to the flag.

By 1837, there were

twenty-six stars on the flag.

By 1850, there were thirty-one.

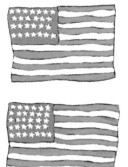

One country.

One flag.

But then in 1861,

something happened.

Our country split in two.

Eleven states in the South

broke away from

the United States of America.

They started their own country.

It was called the Confederate

(you say it like this: con-FED-ur-it)

States of America.

Abraham Lincoln was president

of the United States.

He said <u>all</u> the states

had to stay together.

War broke out—the Civil War.

It was a very sad time

in the history of our country.

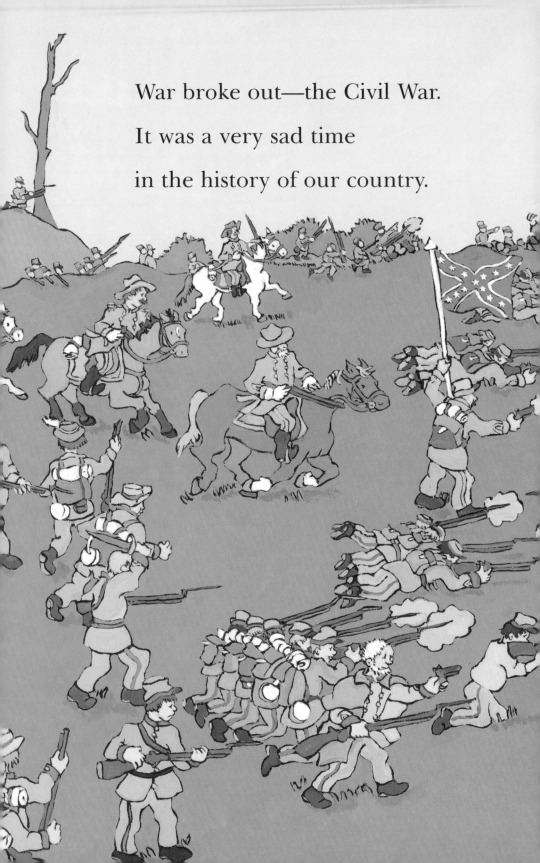

The eleven southern states stopped flying
the Stars and Stripes.
They had their own flag.

In the North, some people wanted eleven

stars taken off the Stars and Stripes.

But Abraham Lincoln would not do that.

He said the states would

get back together.

He was right.

The Civil War ended in 1865.

The North won.

And the United States

was one country under one flag again.

On June 14, 1877, the flag
had a birthday—a big one.
It was 100 years old.

All across the country,
people had picnics
and parties and parades.
June 14 became a holiday—
Flag Day.

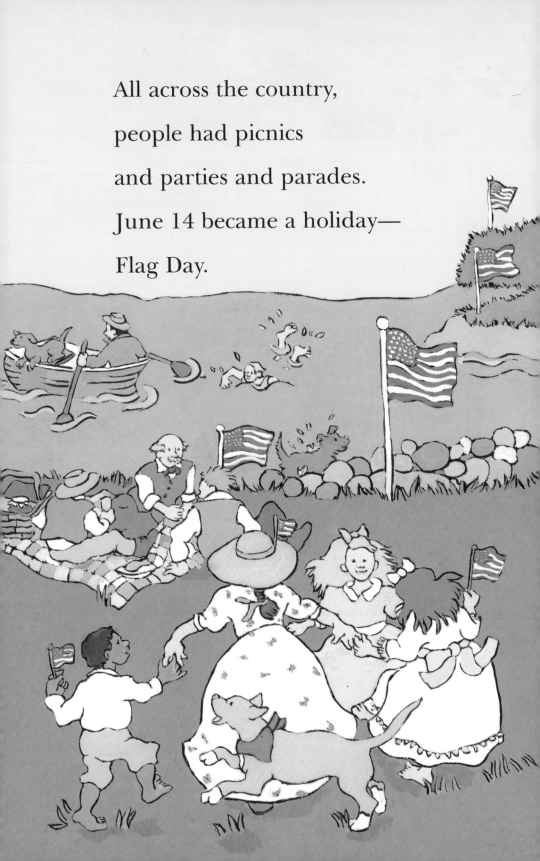

Today our flag has fifty stars
for the fifty United States of America.
Some flags are huge.

One weighs 500 pounds!
It is flown every Fourth of July
from the George Washington Bridge.

The American flag flies

in towns and cities

from coast to coast.

And that's not all.

In 1969, two American astronauts

were the first people ever

to land on the moon.

The astronauts took

lots of moon rocks

back to Earth.

They also left something

on the moon . . .

the Stars and Stripes.

And do you know what?

Our flag is still flying there!

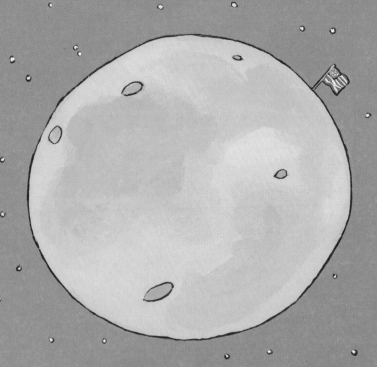